Dear Parent:
Your child's love of reading starts here!

Every child learns to read in a different way and at his or her own speed. Some go back and forth between reading levels and read favorite books again and again. Others read through each level in order. You can help your young reader improve and become more confident by encouraging his or her own interests and abilities. From books your child reads with you to the first books he or she reads alone, there are I Can Read Books for every stage of reading:

SHARED READING
Basic language, word repetition, and whimsical illustrations, ideal for sharing with your emergent reader

BEGINNING READING
Short sentences, familiar words, and simple concepts for children eager to read on their own

READING WITH HELP
Engaging stories, longer sentences, and language play for developing readers

READING ALONE
Complex plots, challenging vocabulary, and high-interest topics for the independent reader

ADVANCED READING
Short paragraphs, chapters, and exciting themes for the perfect bridge to chapter books

I Can Read Books have introduced children to the joy of reading since 1957. Featuring award-winning authors and illustrators and a fabulous cast of beloved characters, I Can Read Books set the standard for beginning readers.

A lifetime of discovery begins with the magical words **"I Can Read!"**

Visit www.icanread.com for information
on enriching your child's reading experience.

Paddington and the Magic Trick Text copyright © 2016 by Michael Bond. Story adapted by Christy Webster from an original Paddington story written by Michael Bond. Illustrations copyright © 2016 by HarperCollins Publishers. All rights reserved. Manufactured in China. No part of this book may be used or reproduced in any manner whatsoever without written permission except in the case of brief quotations embodied in critical articles and reviews. For information address HarperCollins Children's Books, a division of HarperCollins Publishers, 195 Broadway, New York, NY 10007.
www.icanread.com

Library of Congress Control Number: 2015943983
ISBN 978-0-06-243068-7 (trade bdg.) — ISBN 978-0-06-243067-0 (pbk.)

Typography by Rick Farley

PADDINGTON
and the Magic Trick

Michael Bond
illustrated by R. W. Alley

HARPER
An Imprint of HarperCollinsPublishers

It was Paddington's first birthday
since moving in with the Browns.
Everyone was getting ready
for the party.
Judy hung streamers.
Jonathan blew up balloons.

Paddington could hardly contain
his excitement.

Mrs. Bird baked a special cake
for the big day.
She filled it with marmalade
and covered it with icing.

Paddington wanted a taste.

Mrs. Bird let him lick the spoon.

It was the best birthday cake

he'd ever tasted!

Paddington went to look

at his presents.

He opened his new magic set.

He put on the hat and cape.

Paddington had a great idea!

He would perform at the party.

But first he had to learn

a few magic tricks.

Paddington waved the magic wand.

"Abracadabra!" he said.

He did not see his marmalade jar

drop into the secret drawer.

The trick worked!

Paddington practiced some more.

He couldn't wait to perform

for his guests.

Soon the guests arrived.

Paddington's good friend,

Mr. Gruber, led the way.

Everyone sang "Happy Birthday."
Then Paddington blew out
the candles on his cake.

It was time for the magic show.

Paddington set up

his magic box.

Jonathan and Judy
dimmed the lights.
Everyone was excited
to see Paddington perform.

Paddington put an egg

on the magic box.

He covered it with a scarf.

He said the magic word.

He waved his wand.

The egg had disappeared!

Paddington took a bow.

He tucked his paw

into the secret drawer

to get the egg.

Ta-da! It was . . . a jar.

Paddington was surprised.

How had a jar

ended up where the egg

was supposed to be?

Paddington's guests smiled

and waited for the next trick.

Next Paddington would make

flowers disappear.

But he could not remember

all the steps.

Paddington opened a large door
in the back of the box.

He crawled inside to check
the steps in his magic book.

His guests waited and waited.

Was this the trick?

Finally, Mr. Gruber

knocked on the box.

"Are you okay in there, Mr. Brown?"

Paddington was stuck!

Mr. Brown helped Paddington
out of the box.
"Maybe you could do
another kind of magic trick,"
Mrs. Brown suggested.

27

Paddington tried a card trick.

Mr. Gruber picked a card.

Paddington tore it
into little pieces.

"This part is tricky,"
said Paddington.
He covered the card
with his scarf.

Paddington waved the wand.

"Abracadabra!" he said.

"Oh!" said Mr. Gruber.

"The trick worked!"

He put his hand behind his ear

and pulled out a coin.

Mr. Gruber handed him the coin.

Paddington knew just how

he would spend it.

He would buy their next

morning buns!